ESSENTIAL ZEN HABITS

ESSENTIAL ZEN HABITS

MASTERING THE ART
OF CHANGE,
BRIEFLY

Leo Babauta

Uncopyright

FOR MY DAD, JOSE BABAUTA, WHOSE PASSION
FOR THE TRUTH OF ART INSPIRED WHO I AM.
AND FOR MY FRIEND SCOTT DINSMORE,
WHO ALWAYS DREAMED BIG.
I MISS YOU BOTH.

Contents

❀ Part I ❀
Creating a Habit

✤ Part II ✤
Habit Troubleshooting

✤ Part III ✤
Quitting a Bad Habit

✿ Part IV ✿
Life Struggles

✿ Part V ✿
Just Do This

Introduction:
The only reason we struggle
with habit change

*The art of life lies in a constant
readjustment to our surroundings.*

OKAKURA KAKUZO

There's a projector in our minds, and it's constantly playing a movie about how we'd like things to be, our ideals about the world, our expectations of how things will turn out, how others should be, how we should be. These images aren't based on reality, but are just a fantasy this film projector has created from nothing.

It turns out that this fantasy, which I call the Mind Movie, is what stands in our way of making habit changes. As well-intentioned as the mind is when it creates this fantasy, it's also causing us frustration, struggle, bad feelings about ourselves, procrastination, distraction, and more. In other words, this Mind Movie is at the heart of all of our problems.

Creating a new habit, for example, should be a pretty simple task. In theory. It's simply repeating an action after a trigger (say, the habit of writing after the trigger of your morning coffee) over and over until it becomes more and more automatic. If you do the action after the trigger every day for about six weeks, you should have a fairly automatic habit. Do it for several months, and it'll be pretty ingrained in your life.

So if it's so simple, why do we struggle to create new habits and drop old bad habits? Because the mind is like a little child—constantly seeking comfort and pleasure and control. This Childish Mind is playing a Mind Movie all the time, about how our lives should be so comfortable and pleasurable and orderly. The mind then runs from discomfort and fear and change and confusion, which aren't at all the fantasy playing in the Mind Movie.

Unfortunately, creating a new habit or dropping an old habit can't be done without discomfort. When we change our usual way of doing things, this becomes uncomfortable—sometimes to a really strong degree. The Mind Movie tells us that changing a habit should be easy and fun, but the reality is that we must wander outside our comfort zone. And so the Childish Mind rebels. It throws a tantrum.

This Mind Movie and the rebellion of the Childish Mind is not just at the heart of our struggles with habit change; it's at the heart of all our struggles. When we procrastinate on the important work we want to do, when we avoid pursuing our creative dreams because of fear of failure, when we struggle with healthy eating and exercise, when we are frustrated with other people or ourselves or our life situation ... these struggles are a result of the Childish Mind and the Mind Movie.

How I changed my life

I struggled for many years with health problems, procrastination, debt, being stuck in jobs I didn't like, never pursuing my dreams, being overweight, not being able to quit smoking or junk food. I struggled with the Childish Mind and the Mind Movie, and didn't realize why I was struggling. What was wrong with me?

I tried many times to change all my habits, sometimes succeeding for a week or two, but always ending in failure and guilt. I'd end up just feeling worse about myself.

I finally overcame this cycle of failure and guilt by completely focusing myself on one habit change (quitting smoking), and not letting my Childish Mind run away from the discomfort. It was a massive struggle, but I learned that I didn't need to listen to this Childish Mind, that it would raise hell but ultimately all the complaining was just noise.

I proved to myself that I could overcome the resistance, and I learned to turn from the Mind Movie to embrace the reality in front of me. The moment in front of me was awesome.

I also learned to change habits in tiny steps, gradually, so that the Childish Mind wouldn't rebel so violently. One at a time, I changed my eating habits slowly over long periods of time. One change at a time, I was able to start running, start writing in the morning, start a business, start paying off my debt and saving and investing, start getting rid of clutter. I became a minimalist, a published author, a vegan, a marathoner, and more.

All from learning to deal with the Childish Mind.

I'd like to share what I've learned with you, in this small volume of distilled methods. I challenge you to work with me on these skills over the next 6 weeks.

How this book works

I wrote a longer version of this book in 2014, but for this second edition, I decided to toss out those carefully crafted chapters with their stories and longish explanations. For this edition, I wanted no fluff, just the essentials.

So, with inspiration from a blog post by author Derek Sivers (sivers.org), I've decided to compress this book into a series of "Just Do This" instructions. I'll explain the instructions, but I won't go into detailed reasoning or stories. I'll assume you're ready to make a change, and you trust me to tell you what I've found to work. I'll assume you're going to do your best to implement the instructions.

In return, you'll get everything I've learned about changing habits and dealing with struggle in a compact volume that you can read in minutes a day, or all in one day if you wanted.

You can read it however you like, but I recommend that you:

1. Set aside 10 minutes every morning, and read one chapter a day.

2. Create one new habit for the next six weeks (not quit an old habit).

3. Follow the weekly focuses that I set out in this book, for your new habit.

4. Then read through the Troubleshooting, Quitting a Bad Habit and Life Struggles sections.

5. Finally, wrap it all up with the Just Do This section at the end, which will distill all of this book into a few pages of brief instructions.

In this book, I'll give you a method for dealing with the Childish Mind and the Mind Movie. If you practice the method over the next six weeks and beyond, it will help you not only become better at changing habits, but dealing with procrastination and life struggles.

This book isn't about how to make yourself a better person—it's about how to remove the things that get in your way.

The Challenge: Commit to making a small change

I hereby issue a challenge to you: Commit to reading one brief section of this book every day (usually the daily missions, just a paragraph each), and commit to making one small change in your life as you read this book (but don't start the change yet!).

Each section is short and the missions in the chapters are easy, and all together the reading and missions should take about 10 minutes a day.

This challenge is essential to this book: if you put the ideas into action, you'll learn them through practice. If you just read the book without acting (which you are probably tempted to do), you're wasting your time.

So: are you up for the challenge? If you are, make a decision this minute to make one small change as you read this book. Be all in. Don't start until Day 6 of the Week 1 chapter, but today you can make a strong commitment to yourself.

Key Concepts to Know

Instead of doing a chapter on each of these ideas, here are the
key concepts you'll see throughout this book:

1. MIND MOVIE: The fantasy your mind plays in its head
   about how things should be. This fantasy might be
   about how nice your life would be if you had a meditation habit, or ate healthily, or got fit with Crossfit. The
   fantasy might be about how disciplined or productive or
   mindful you should be. It might be about how consider-
   ate other people should be to you, or how they should
   ideally behave, or how great your life should be. These
   fantasies aren't true, but your mind believes them any-
   way, because it really wants them to be true. It feels like
   they should be real. Unfortunately, these Mind Movies
   get in our way of appreciating life and making healthy
   changes, and they create struggle for us.
2. CHILDISH MIND: The part of our mind that com-
   plains about how things are, that fears discomfort, that
   just wants pleasure and comfort, that doesn't want
   things to be difficult. This is like a little child who
   throws a tantrum every time he doesn't get his way.

We all have this Childish Mind, and in this book we'll learn to deal with this part of ourselves.

3. MINDFULNESS: In this book, we'll use the term "mindfulness" not as a general term for living in the moment, but to refer to two methods: 1) turning inward and seeing the Mind Movie, the Childish Mind's resistance, the urge to quit, the feeling we're having difficulty with; and 2) turning from the Mind Movie to the reality that's in front of us, and finding appreciation for that reality.

4. GROUNDLESSNESS: I stole the concept of "groundlessness" from Buddhist teacher Pema Chodron. It describes the feeling of not having solid ground under your feet—for example, when you lose your job or a loved one dies, and you feel like the rug has been pulled out from under you. You are adrift at sea, without an anchor. And in fact, this happens to us all the time, in big and small ways. Any time we're feeling resistance, dissatisfaction, frustration, sadness, uncertainty, fear, doubt, loss, unhappiness with ourselves ... this is a form of groundlessness. In this book, we'll look at ways of dealing with the dissatisfaction and groundlessness that pervade our lives.

5. RESISTANCE: When we procrastinate or fail to follow our exercise plan, we do so because of resistance. It's the Childish Mind complaining about having to do something, about a situation, about someone else ... because that person, task or situation doesn't match the Mind Movie, isn't comfortable. We're going to learn to deal with this resistance, which is of course another form of groundlessness.

6. SELF-COMPASSION: We've all found compassion for other people—a wish for their suffering or dissatisfaction to end, for them to find peace, happiness, contentment. This is a beautiful wish, and it makes us feel and act more kindly toward others. In this book, we'll try to practice this compassion with ourselves, as a way to deal with the Childish Mind, dissatisfaction, and resistance.

7. INTENTION: When you set to do something—let's say write a book, or have a conversation with someone—you can set an intention before you do that activity, as a way of consciously deciding what you're hoping to do during the activity. For example, you might have the intention of compassionately helping people as you write your book. This doesn't mean you actually think things will turn out this way (you might not help anyone), but it means you're bringing the intention of helping into the activity. This intention informs your approach, and how you feel and act during the activity.

These short summaries of the key ideas of this book are just an introduction. We'll expand on them as we work through the book.

❀ PART I ❀
Creating a Habit

In this section, we'll work together to create a new habit over the next six weeks. We'll cover the basics by focusing on one key area each week, with daily missions. By the end of this section, you should know how to create a new habit, and be able to practice these steps with future habits.

How to choose a first habit

You're not going to choose a habit today to work with in this book, but we should talk about good habits to choose. The habit needs to be easy, a new habit (not quitting an old habit), and something you can do once a day.

That would be an ideal habit to start with, because you won't face as much resistance as a very difficult habit (difficult exercise routines, for example) or quitting an ingrained habit (like smoking or Internet addictions).

For example, here are a few ideas for good habits to work on:

· Walk for 5 minutes
· Do 10 pushups
· Drink tea in the morning
· Meditate for a few minutes
· Write a couple paragraphs a day
· Sketch something simple
· Journal
· Eat a vegetable with lunch
· Find 5 pieces of clutter to recycle/donate

· Drink a glass of water in the morning
· Put clothes in hamper after you shower

Notice that none of these is that difficult (if any seems difficult, don't choose it). What you don't want to choose is something hard like "clear email inbox every morning" or "declutter entire house in a week" or "eat all vegetables and whole foods, no junk." These are much harder to do, and not good habits to pick right now.

Quitting habits vs. starting a positive habit

Another type of habit not to choose right now is the negative habit: not doing something (like not checking social media) or quitting a bad habit (like smoking or shopping). We'll get to these types of habits in the Quitting Habits section later, but for now, choose a positive action ("do 10 push-ups") rather than a negative ("don't give in to distractions"). If someone can see you doing the action, that's a positive habit.

The reason is that quitting old habits is a bit more complicated. Quitting requires all the same steps as starting a new positive habit, but also requires you to deal with the urges and resistance of quitting the old habit. So it's a more advanced practice, and it's better to start with the basics first.

Two questions before you start

These are two common questions that come up as people do the steps in the following chapters.

Q: WHY ARE THERE SIX DAYS IN EACH OF THE WEEKS IN THE FOLLOWING CHAPTER?
A: I don't want to overwhelm you with too much to do, so I made each day quick to read and easy to do, and gave you a day off each week. But if you miss a day, you can use the day off to catch up if you like.

Q: WHAT IF I MISS A DAY OF DOING THE HABIT?
A: That's totally normal! Practice the technique of not attaching to the Mind Movie of doing it perfectly, but instead just learn from what happened and keep going. The most important thing is to keep going. Don't quit just because you missed a day or three.

I highly recommend that you practice expecting imperfection. You won't do this habit perfectly—no one does. So expect to mess up, consider it a part of the process, and just enjoy the journey.

Week 1 focus: A slow start

Over the next 6 weeks, I am challenging you to stick with one daily habit, with a different focus each week, and missions six days of every week. Don't start doing your habit yet. This week's focus is "A Slow Start," and we'll be preparing to start the habit and then starting as easily as possible. Try to do one mission a day, with a day of rest each week. Note: If you miss multiple days, that's OK, just keep going and pick up where you left off—we're not on a deadline.

Day 1: Pick one change

Today I'd like you to simply pick a new habit to work on. Refer back to the last chapter, "How to choose a first habit," for some guidelines on choosing a good habit. Think about something that would be easy, but a positive, meaningful change. Something you actually care about, and that feels connected to a purpose that's important to you. Don't start on it yet, until Day 6!

Day 2: Create a vow

Today, consider your intention with this new habit. Why are you doing it? Does this reason feel important to you, connected to one of your deeper purposes? Is it a compassionate act for yourself or others? Understand your reason, and set an intention. Now make a big commitment to yourself—be all in, and vow not to let yourself down. Write this vow down somewhere you can see it each day, and honor yourself by sticking to this vow to your utmost ability.

Day 3: Make it small

We made a big vow, now we're going to make the habit as small as possible. We're not going to start yet, but today, I'd like you to consider how to make this habit as easy as possible once you get started. Can you cut it down to just one minute each day? For example, if your habit is meditation or writing, can you say that for the first week or so, you'll just try to do one minute a day? You're going to expand it once you get into the rhythm, but to start with, just consider how small you can make the habit.

Day 4: Create a space

Today, I'd like you to create space to focus on the change you're going to make. If this habit is to be a priority, you need to set aside some time. When will you do it? I prefer doing it in the mornings, because if it's important, you want it to come before all the busywork you need to do, but you'll need to figure out when is best for you. Make this a priority, and set aside at least 10 minutes to do this habit—even if you're only going to do it for a minute to start with, it's good to have a cushion. Consider this a sacred 10-minute space, which can't be violated by checking things online or other busywork. During this time, you'll only focus on your habit and these missions.

Day 5: Set a trigger & reminder

In the introduction, I mentioned the idea of a trigger—something already in your routine you're going to tie the habit to. A new habit, to become automatic, must be bonded to a trigger. By repeating the trigger-habit sequence over and over, you create a heartbeat rhythm (ba-pum, ba-pum!) that becomes ingrained in your mind. So today, before you start the habit, find a trigger that you already do each day. If you don't think you have a routine, you might write down everything you do in the morning and see if there's something on that list that you do every day. Some possibilities: morning coffee, opening your laptop, taking a shower, brushing your teeth, waking up, getting to work, getting home from work, eating breakfast (or lunch or dinner), going to bed. After you've picked a trigger, write out a reminder on a piece of paper and put it near where the trigger happens (near the coffeemaker if the trigger is drinking coffee). This reminder will be useful when you start doing the habit tomorrow.

Day 6: Start easy

Today's the day you actually start the habit, at last! To start, I'd like you to do what I call the Minimum Viable Habit—the smallest version of the habit, which doesn't limit you to doing more, but is the bare minimum you need for success. For the next week or so, do the habit for just one minute or so, right after your trigger. Yes, doing it for a minute will seem silly, but it's important to make the habit as easy as possible for the first week, to overcome the resistance of the Childish Mind. This is the strategy I used to start the running habit—all I needed to do for my Minimum Viable Habit was lace up my shoes and get out the door. That was so easy I couldn't say no. As you do your habit, try to mindfully enjoy it, and then congratulate yourself on sticking to your vow! You should also do the habit on Day 7 if you can, focusing on just starting the habit.

Week 2 focus:
Mindful enjoyment

This week, we're going to continue to do the habit for just a minute a day, but the focus will be on mindfulness, gratitude, and enjoyment as you do the habit each day. Try to do the habit every day this week.

Day 1: Enjoy the habit

There's a tendency to treat a habit like a chore, and rush to move on to the next thing you need to do. Notice the rush to move on, and instead, try to slow down and enjoy the habit. Smile. Enjoy the learning process, and reflect on the sense of accomplishment when you're done doing the habit. The more you can give yourself this positive feedback during the habit change process, the better, because positive reinforcement is what keeps you doing the habit over time.

Day 2: Be mindful of your movie

As you do your habit today, reflect on what your Mind Movie is about the habit. What ideal or fantasy do you have about this habit? What story are you telling yourself about it? Now turn your attention to the reality of doing the habit, and be curious about what the habit is actually like.

Day 3: Focus on gratitude

Continue your curiosity and exploration of what the habit is actually like, in reality, as opposed to in your Mind Movie. Search for little things to appreciate about that reality. Smile, and find gratitude for those little things, and the opportunity to practice this habit. Gratitude is a great antidote to resistance that we can practice each day, including when our Childish Mind eventually starts to rebel against doing the habit.

Day 4: Practice mindfully

For the minute or so that you do your habit today, practice shining the spotlight of mindfulness onto the habit. Turn the spotlight onto your breath, then your body, your surroundings, all the other sensations associated with the movements of doing your habit. Appreciate everything wonderful about the habit so that the habit itself becomes your reward.

Day 5: Reflect and (optionally) journal

Practice doing your habit mindfully again today, finding gratitude and appreciation. When you're done doing the habit, take a minute to reflect on the past week or so of doing the habit. What has it actually been like, as opposed to the fantasy you had about it before you started? What have you learned? What do you appreciate? What obstacles have come up, and are there ways to overcome them as you continue? Consider writing a short journal entry about these reflections, to solidify your learning. Treat habit formation as a learning process, as a way to learn about yourself, your mind, mindfulness, resistance and more.

Day 6: Adjust to a 2-minute habit

If all has gone well this week, and you haven't struggled or skipped the habit for more than a day, I recommend that you lengthen the habit to two minutes a day. If you've struggled, keep it at a minute. These times are the minimum—if you feel inspired, feel free to go a bit longer, but never so long that it becomes difficult. This slow change process of expanding the habit a little at a time helps overcome the resistance of the mind to change and discomfort. Each step isn't difficult, so your mind doesn't rebel much. Gradually the habit becomes your new normal and you can expand a bit more, pushing your comfort zone a little at a time.

Week 3 focus:
Overcoming "the dip"

This week is often the week that people quit doing the habit, even if they were fairly motivated and successful the first couple weeks. Why? The mind gets tired from continuous focus and effort, and wants to quit during this phase that I call "the dip." You might not encounter it this week, but we're still going to discuss the Dip for future habit changes. So do your habit each day this week, and if all is going well, feel free to add two more minutes to your Minimum Viable Habit in the middle of the week (for a total of four to five minutes). If you're struggling, just stay at two minutes.

Day 1: Notice Your Resistance

Watch for any resistance you have doing the habit today, or reflect on recent resistance you've seen in your mind. If you see the urge to do something else, this is the Childish Mind putting up resistance to discomfort. Be curious: What does the resistance feel like? Is there a way to accept the thing you're resisting, accept the discomfort, relax into it, and find gratitude for it? What is good about the discomfort?

Day 2: Flow around missing a day

It's possible you've missed a day of doing your habit … if not, you likely will in the next week or two. When you miss a day or two, you can either feel bad about it and possibly get derailed completely, or you can flow around it and not make it a big deal. There will always be disruptions—due to travel, crises, big work projects, exhaustion, forgetting, illness, other priorities—and these disruptions very often lead to people quitting the habit. A key habit skill is learning to flow around the disruptions and just keep going. Put aside the Mind Movie of doing things perfectly, and instead embrace the new landscape that you need to adjust to. Even if you haven't missed a day yet, start adopting a flow mentality today.

Day 3: Overcome a motivation slump

For the next few days, pay attention to your motivation levels—is it as high now as when you started? If it is dipping, this is probably because the reality of doing the habit for this long isn't matching your Mind Movie. This is a wonderful opportunity to turn from your expectations for this habit, to learning what other things can motivate you besides this particular Mind Movie. Other motivations you might explore: the joy of doing, curiosity, the pride of accomplishment, the feeling of tenacity and sticking with something difficult, the love of learning, a connection with deeper meaning, helping others, practicing mindfulness, learning to push through difficulty. These are all great motivations to explore for any pursuit.

Day 4: Practice self-compassion

If you've been struggling, resisting, uncomfortable, disappointed, feeling like quitting ... these are some forms of dissatisfaction. If you have felt any of these during this habit change, try to practice with these difficult feelings as you do the habit today. Put your attention on how your difficulty feels. Explore the feeling instead of avoiding it. After a minute or two of just keeping your attention on this feeling of struggle, give yourself kindness, as you would comfort a friend who was struggling or in pain. If you haven't struggled with this habit, find other difficult feelings you've been having and practice with them.

Day 5: Reflect again, adjust

Take a minute after practicing your habit to reflect again on the past week of doing the habit. What has the habit been like and how have you done? What have you learned? What are you grateful for? What obstacles have you faced and what can you do to overcome them? Consider writing a short journal entry on these reflections. If you've made any mistakes, improve your method by figuring out where things went wrong, learning from them and making adjustments. Failure then becomes a great teacher.

Day 6: Stay with groundlessness

As we work on a habit, we are faced with groundlessness. We think the habit will go a certain way, but in reality we're constantly getting lost. We are faced with uncertainty, a feeling of wanting to quit, a struggle with not doing it the right way. This is normal. As you do your habit, practice staying with these feelings, rather than trying to avoid them with distraction. Notice the feelings of discomfort and uncertainty, and stay with them. Get to know them. Get intimate with these feelings. This is an ongoing practice you might experiment with in the coming weeks.

Week 4 focus: Reconnecting

This week is about coming back to some of the ideas we have already practiced, refocusing on and reconnecting with them. Continue your habit each day, with this renewed focus.

Day 1: Quit the third time

Notice the urge to quit doing the habit after you start. We normally follow the urge without thinking. Notice the impulse to get up, to stop … and don't follow it. Just watch, but don't act. Pause and notice this urge and then continue doing the habit. The urge will go away, and you'll find that not following it isn't the end of the world. Then when it comes back, once again don't follow it. Notice but just pause, let it go away. And when the urge to quit comes a third time … go ahead and stop. You've earned it, after not following the urge twice. Try doing this "quit on the third time" practice all week.

Day 2: Reconnect with your why

Today we want to pause for a moment to remember our intention for this habit, our deeper reason for doing it. It's good to reconnect with this "why" before doing the habit each day. Think back to the first week, when you set your vow: what was your intention? Why was this important to you? If it's to help yourself, or to help others, consider those people (or that person) now, and keep them in mind as you do the habit.

Day 3: Reconnect with the moment

Reconnect with your intention as you start doing the habit, then turn away from your Mind Movie and to the moment in front of you. It can be like opening your eyes and seeing what's there for the first time, if we've been lost in our thoughts. Look all around you and appreciate the details of your movement and all that surrounds you. Notice the energy of the entire moment. Hold the sense of that energy in your attention for as long as you can. Your attention will fade out, but try to bring it back to the energy of the moment around you. This is another good practice to continue beyond today.

Day 4: Reconnect with gratitude

After reconnecting with your intention and trying to fully experience the moment in front of you, the next practice is to reconnect with the gratitude we focused on in earlier weeks. See if you have gratitude for being in this moment, being able to do this habit, being able to carry our your intention, being alive. This gives us a process to continue practicing each day: set your intention, sense the energy of the moment as you do the habit, feel the gratitude, and only quit on the third urge.

Day 5: On struggles

If you've struggled this week, as you practice the process we discussed yesterday … reflect on these struggles. What Mind Movie are you tightly attached to? What is the Childish Mind rebelling against? How can you give compassion to the resistance of the Childish Mind? How can you turn away from the Mind Movie to find appreciation for the moment, and the habit you're doing? This practice of working with what you're struggling with is crucial as you continue the habit and the process of changing your life.

Day 6: Don't waste life

There's a quote by Stoic philosopher Seneca that moves me and which I encourage you to reflect on today: "You are living as if destined to live forever … you don't notice how much time has already passed, but squander it as though you had a full and overflowing supply—though all the while that very day … may be your last." Seneca also said that "putting things off is the biggest waste of life." Dogen, the great Zen master, also wrote: "Students today should begrudge every moment of time. This dewlike life fades away; time speeds swiftly. In this short life of ours, avoid involvement in superfluous things and just study the Way." This "Way" that he was talking about is studying the nature of change, which is what we're doing as we work on changing this habit. As we finish up this important week, let's reflect on not wasting this precious, dewlike life we've been given, and instead study this habit change as if it were the most important change of our lives.

Week 5 focus:
Embracing groundlessness

This week we're going to continue doing the habit, which is starting to solidify. This week is a good opportunity to practice consistency with the habit. We'll also go deeper into the practice of dealing with struggles and groundlessness we touched on in the last two weeks. We'll learn to embrace this groundlessness, and to be OK with things not being firm and certain or going as we'd like. This is a great practice for habit change, and for life in general.

Day 1: Be curious about groundlessness

When we experience groundlessness—a feeling of not being anchored, not certain, things not going our way, a feeling of loss—our minds don't normally like it. Our minds resist or avoid these feelings. Today I encourage you to be curious about the groundlessness you might feel with your habit, or other recent times when you've felt struggle, loss, uncertainty. Stay with the feeling and examine it with an open mind. Practice becoming more familiar, even intimate with it, all this week.

Day 2: Practice being with uncertainty

Something you've likely felt as you've done your habit, especially at the beginning, is uncertainty about how you're doing the habit. Are you doing it right? Is there more you should know? When will it be ingrained as a habit? These and many more questions pass through our heads as we do a habit, or anything that we don't already know by heart. We tend not to like the feeling of uncertainty, not only with this habit but in other areas of your life. Today, practice just staying with this feeling of uncertainty, seeing what it's like to not know the path, know the right way, know the answer. See if you can just be uncertain, and be curious about what this is like.

Day 3: Practice being with discomfort

One reason exercise is such a difficult habit to form is because of the discomfort it brings. The Childish Mind doesn't like discomfort any more than it likes uncertainty. We have to face discomfort when we deal with a tough work task, when we have to write something, in social situations, or when we put ourselves out there in the world. These are scary, uncomfortable situations. But if we don't push into discomfort, we severely limit ourselves. We limit the kind of work we do, we can make ourselves unhealthy, and we limit our social happiness. So today, consider pushing yourself into discomfort, either with the habit or with something else. Stay with the discomfort, find curiosity about it, see if you can be OK with the uncomfortable feeling without letting your mind run from it.

Day 4: See that this is enough

There's a part of our minds where we're always looking for more. This is true of your current habit—you want it to be better in the future, you want your life (or yourself) to be better—and it's true of many other things in your life. Are your friends, family, spouse, kids, yourself, your work, your body ... enough as they are? Or do you have a Mind Movie about how they should be? As you do your habit today, notice your mind's tendency to move to what you need to do today, things coming in the future ... and pause. Stop and see the energy of the entire current moment, your own energy included. And practice accepting this moment as already enough. This is a good practice to carry forward through your day, and beyond this week.

Day 5: Practice letting go & accepting

One of the most difficult tasks we can give to our Childish Mind is letting go of what it really wants, and accepting life as it is, seeing that it's already enough. What is it that you really want, when it comes to this habit? Is it possible to become unattached to that desire, to let it go and live without it? Would life be enough? There will be times when life forces us to live without what we want (the death of a loved one, for example), and we struggle to let go. Other times, when we aren't forced to let go, we hold on and it can make us unhealthy. We'll be much better prepared for these situations if we practice with our habit today, and other days as well, with letting go of what we really want and accepting that the moment in front of us is already enough.

Day 6: Go through to love

What happens when we stay with groundlessness (uncertainty, discomfort, frustration, loss), and don't run from it? Is there just the discomfort of groundlessness, or is there anything beneath that? According to my teacher, Zen priest Susan O'Connell of San Francisco Zen Center, the answer is love. When we are frustrated with someone, it's because we love them. When we are afraid because of uncertainty, the fear comes from a place of love, underneath it all. I believe there's truth to this, but I encourage you to stay with your groundlessness, explore it for as long as you can, and see if you can peek beneath it to see what's there.

◆

Week 6 focus:
Gradually changing your life

We've covered the basics of creating habits and dealing with struggles. This week we'll take some time to solidify our habit while considering ideas for creating new habits. Continue your habit as usual with the practices we've discussed, as we talk about these new ideas.

Day 1: Consider a second habit

If your new habit is becoming ingrained, you might be eager to start a new habit. This is a great impulse. It's usually a mistake to try to do two habits at once, but once the first habit has become part of your new "normal," you can think about a second habit. I recommend considering another positive habit that is meaningful to your deeper purposes. You'll want to go back to Week 1's instructions and start all over with the second habit, after this week is over.

Day 2: Gradually change your life

If you started your first habit small and progressed gradually, you've learned the Slow Change method. Instead of revamping your entire diet all at once, imagine adding one vegetable each week, then a fruit, then nuts, and slowly, gradually, your entire diet changes. It's gradual, so you barely notice the difference, and your Childish Mind hardly objects. Today, consider whether you did the Slow Change method with your first habit, and consider what tiny changes you can make over the next few months that will be easy to make but meaningful in the long term.

Day 3: Let go of unhelpful changes

The gradual change of your life sometimes means letting go of habit changes that haven't worked out well. I had a friend who diligently stuck to a yoga habit almost every morning for more than two months, but just wasn't enjoying the habit. It wasn't adding joy to his life, so he eventually dropped it. It can be disappointing to let go of a habit you had such high hopes for and worked so long for, but we have to remember that we do these habit changes to learn about ourselves. One thing we might learn is that this habit isn't as helpful as we'd imagined. No matter what the outcome, we've learned a lot through the process. Today, consider whether your new habit has been as helpful as you'd pictured … and whether it's worth carrying it forward. If not, give yourself permission to drop it, and perhaps revisit the habit later.

Day 4: Adjust & refocus

If you decide to keep your habit going, now consider how it has gone, what you've learned, and what obstacles you've encountered. What adjustments do you need to make? What have you learned that can be applied to future habits? It's a good idea to write a short journal entry to solidify these learnings. Finally, refocus yourself on the deeper Why of the habit, the intention and the gratitude you've practiced with, as you go forward.

Day 5: Go into habit maintenance mode

As you prepare to take on a second habit, you'll want to continue with the first habit by putting it in "habit maintenance mode." This is a way of continuing it with less of a focus. By now, the habit should start to become more automatic if you've been at least a little consistent. You don't need reminders to start, and it's feeling a bit easier, more a part of your "normal." So as you start putting your focus on your second habit, all you want to do is not forget about the first habit. You don't need to keep track of it every day, as long as things are going well. Every few days, pause and reflect on your first habit and check in to see that everything is still going well. Maybe once a week, use one of these reflection sessions to assess whether you have any obstacles around the first habit, need to make adjustments, learned anything new. After awhile, you need to reflect on the habit less often, as it becomes ingrained in your life.

Day 6: Embrace the uncertain path of change

The truth is, the path to changing your habits and the gradual changing of your life won't be straight, ordered, neat. It will be messy, littered with failed habits, with constant stops and restarts. There isn't an optimal path or certainty that you're doing it right. I've never experienced that and don't know anyone who set out with a habit plan for 12 months and accomplished it exactly. It's much messier. So if you're hoping for a plan with certainty and precision, you'll need to toss out that Mind Movie, and instead embrace the uncertainty of not knowing what the hell you're doing. See if you can stay in this place of uncertainty, continue to walk down the path of habit change without anyone telling you it's the right way, and be OK with it. You've practiced with uncertainty, discomfort and groundlessness for at least a few weeks now, and your path is to continue that practice. Embrace the uncertain path with curiosity.

❦ PART II ❦
Habit Troubleshooting

This section of the book is meant for you to refer to if you have any trouble with your habit, or future habits. It's not a bad idea to skim through these short chapters even if you're not having trouble, just so you'll know to come back here if problems come up later. Everyone has trouble sometimes—here's a practical guide to dealing with those troubles.

Missed a few days & struggling

It can be difficult to stay consistent with a habit if you have a lot going on in your life, or if the habit is more difficult than you expected. Missing days can cause struggle, and a feeling of not being disciplined. Here are some recommendations—you don't need to do all of these, but you might try one or two, or combine multiple tactics as needed.

Gauge your bandwidth

It's a good idea to take a look at what is going on in your life—do you have a big work project, a lot of work stress, travel, illness, family crises, busy-ness with your family or friends? Are you overwhelmed, stressed out? Any one or more of these factors can cause you to have low bandwidth for creating new habits, and messing up on habits in this case does not reflect on your discipline levels. Consider either taking a break from the habit, or reducing what else you're doing in your life.

Assess your focus & commitment

Even if you don't have a lot going on, it's possible you're not fully focused on this habit, or fully committed to it. Take an assessment of how committed you feel to this habit. How much focus have you been giving it? Can you increase either? What do you need to do to make that happen? Some suggestions follow.

Make a commitment to others

If making a commitment to yourself isn't working, you can increase the commitment by telling others that you're going to create this new habit. Tell your family, friends, co-workers. Announce it on social media. Post it up on a sign in your house or office. By announcing it to others, you might feel more committed. Note that there's a possibility that you'll feel a sense of accomplishment just by announcing it—you'll need to do more than an announcement to create the habit.

Make a rule: Don't miss two days in a row

Missing a day of doing the habit isn't a big deal, but if you miss a second day, it can sometimes trigger a downward spiral. You might feel bad about missing two days, making it likely you'll miss a third day, and feel so bad that you just avoid thinking about the habit. To avoid this downward spiral, you might create a new rule for yourself: never miss two days in a row. When you miss one day, do everything you can to figure out why you missed, and solve it so you don't keep missing.

Create accountability

Making a public commitment to make a change is sometimes only half the equation—to really be motivated, you might also need to report back on how you're doing. Make a promise to report regularly to a group of people, via email, on social media, in person, through an online spreadsheet. Tell them how often you'll report: daily, weekly, monthly. If you make a rule not to miss two days in a row, let them know that. If you create a consequence (see below), tell them about that. Be serious about this commitment to be accountable, report regularly, and you'll see progress.

Create a consequence

In combination with public accountability or the "don't miss two days in a row" rule, you might try creating a fun but embarrassing consequence for missing two days in a row and commit to this with your accountability partner or group. For example, promise to donate to a political campaign or charity that you don't like. Or promise to sing a song and post a recording online. Or, as I did, promise to allow your friend to throw a pie in your face, and put the recording of that online. These consequences shouldn't hurt, but are just fun ways to make you really want to stick to your rule or commitment.

Make it social

You might also do the habit with someone else, or a small group of people. For example, you could do your walking habit with a spouse or friend, or do bodyweight workouts in the park with several friends. You could have a reading group, to form the reading habit, where you check in each day and then discuss the books you're reading weekly or monthly. When you do the habit with others, it can be a lot of fun, and creates motivation.

Can't find the time

When people say they haven't had the time to focus on the habit change, what they really mean is they either 1) don't have the bandwidth, or 2) haven't made it a priority. See the previous chapter for more bandwidth recommendations, but one way of dealing with this is to make the habit as small as possible, so it's hard to say "no" to the habit. Cut the habit down to one or two minutes, and you can't say you don't have the time.

Note that this solution helps overcome a number of habit obstacles: not having enough time, not having enough energy, being overwhelmed or afraid of the change—which is why small changes are so incredibly important for overcoming obstacles.

But if the problem is one of priority—maybe other things need to take priority in your life for awhile—you have a couple options:

1. Take a break from the habit, but make it a defined break—three days, seven days, etc.—and set up a commitment to someone else to start once the break is over.

2. Or don't take a break, but instead learn to make your habit change a priority at all times. Go back to your Minimal Viable Habit (the smallest version of your habit), if things are getting overwhelming.

Another suggestion is to not to let your Childish Mind talk you out of the change, because of fear or discomfort. Often the mind will rationalize not doing the habit because it is tired, or doesn't want to face discomfort, and instead it wants to go to the comfort of distraction. Be prepared for this by anticipating its objections, like not having time today or not feeling up to it, and having your answers ready.

Others aren't supporting me

If we have other people in our lives, sometimes we're lucky and they support us. But often they resist the habit changes we make. Sometimes their unhealthy habits stand in our way. You're trying to eat healthy foods, and yet your daughter would rather eat snack crackers, pizza and cookies than asparagus.

There's no simple answer. We shouldn't abandon our attempts at change, nor is it helpful to try to force change on loved ones. This can be one of the toughest obstacles, because we don't have complete control over others. We can't force other people to be supportive.

What works? Let's take a look at some strategies. Try one, two, or all of them, and figure out what works in your life.

Get others on board

As early as possible, Include everyone in the thinking process about your change—all the people who will be affected by the change (your spouse, kids, friends). Talk to them when you first hear or read about the idea, not after you're ready to make the change. Give them a chance to overcome their resistance, rather than springing the decision on them.

Talk about why it's appealing to you. Get their input. Talk about your motivation for wanting to do this. Include them every step of the way until the decision is made, and after.

What people don't like is being forced to change against their will. So try never to make people feel pressured. Don't ask them to change; ask them to help you change, once you've gotten to the decision. Say that their support is really important to you, and explain that while they are welcome to join you, they don't have to change. Ask them to be your accountability buddy, someone to call on when you inevitably face trouble.

Accept others as they are

When you make a change, others in your life might unconsciously see this change as threatening. A helpful approach is to make it clear that you're not judging what they do, but rather trying to reduce your own struggles with this change. Try to make it clear that you accept them as they are (and try to really accept them).

How can you accept the bad habits of others? Well, put yourself in their place. Have you ever had bad habits? (Of course, we all have.) You didn't like being criticized or attacked, and you appreciated being accepted. This is how the other person feels, and if you don't accept their bad habit, you're not accepting them, and they're likely to resent you and be unsupportive.

So instead, let go of your Mind Movie of how they should be. See the reality of the other person as they are, the love within them, and find something to appreciate about them. Once they feel accepted, they're much less likely to be defensive and much more likely to support you.

Set the example

I've found the best method of persuasion is being a good model for change. It doesn't result in instant persuasion, but over time, people see the changes you're making, see that it's not threatening them, and see the benefits of your changes. Inspire people to consider something they wouldn't normally consider, just by setting a good example. No one else will do yoga with you? That's OK ... keep doing it, and share your experiences (without being annoying).

Make changes on your own

If others won't get on board with your changes, ask just that they give you the space to make the change on your own, without their help. This isn't a small thing sometimes—others can be threatened by your changes, or dislike the disruption of their routine that you're causing. Ask for the space to do it alone, and ask that they not criticize or make it hard on you. If they are resentful, this makes it more difficult, but you'll have to make an effort to show that this is something that will make you happy.

You need to find encouragement elsewhere—find other people in real life or online who are making similar changes. Often there are groups online or in your area where you can meet people in person who are going through the same changes.

Educate with patience

When others opposed my changes, it was often because they didn't understand them. What has helped is education with patience. When they ask questions or criticize, see that as an opportunity to talk about the change, to help them understand. This is a great gift, this opportunity, so talk with them in a way that isn't pushy or trying to prove that you're right, but shows how excited you are and how you'd like to share what you're learning about.

You might also want to share books, websites and blogs you're reading about the topic. Don't share in a way that hints that they should change, but just to show what you're interested in and how they might learn more if they're interested. You can't force people to read or watch, but you can make information available.

Have patience. Don't expect others to understand immediately just because you get it. Don't attach to the result of getting their understanding, but focus on the intention of being patient and helpful. They might not want to support your change at all, at first ... but later, they might come around.

Group challenges

One of my more successful strategies is creating challenges for my family. They aren't required to do the challenges, of course, but sometimes people like the opportunity to rise to a challenge. And they like making changes with others. My wife and I have created eating challenges to do with each other, and with our kids; I've challenged them to do push-ups, handstands, running, vegetarian experiments, daily drawing, writing, and more. Challenges are fun if you do them together. It can be fun to do it as a competition, or to offer rewards for people who complete the challenge.

Not doing as well as I'd hoped

Often we have a Mind Movie of how the habit will go, how beautiful it will be in our lives. This can cause disappointment, frustration, and discouragement when things don't go as we'd hoped.

A good practice is to not attach to the outcome. Have a good intention for the habit, but don't worry too much about how it will turn out, because you can't control that. It's like a plant—you can plant the seeds, water it, nourish it, care for it, but you can't control exactly how it will turn out. So plant the seed of intention, give the intention as much of your loving care as you can, and then let go of how it will turn out.

As you do the habit, be mindful of your attachment to outcomes of this habit, and see if you can focus instead on the intention, on the effort, on enjoying the process.

Accountability isn't working

You might have tried to set up some accountability, as mentioned in the "Missed a few days & struggling" chapter, but perhaps it's not going as you'd planned.

Here are some ideas for accountability and consequences you can create for yourself:

- Publicly commit to doing a habit every day, on social media, to your friends and family.
- Write a daily blog, with short updates.
- Commit to friends and family via a mass email, and promise them weekly updates.
- Create a public log of your habit, and share it with people.
- Join an accountability group and commit to them.
- Find an accountability partner and create consequences for each other if you fail.
- Make a big pledge to do something embarrassing if you fail.
- Make a pledge to give money to someone or to a political candidate or non-profit organization you don't like.

- Pledge to ban yourself from your computer or cell phone, for a few days or a week, if you fail; or not eat sugar or drink coffee or drink wine, or whatever would motivate you most.
- Issue a public challenge to friends to join you in a month-long habit (like writing every day, or exercising each day).
- Get a coach or join a small class.

By creating accountability, we're creating an environment that helps to keep us on the habit path when our minds begin resisting the path.

Feeling tired, stressed, overwhelmed

When your stress levels are high or energy levels are very low, it's hard to maintain any kind of discipline. You just want to relax.

Fortunately, there are ways to overcome this.

1. FIRST, BE AWARE OF THE PROBLEM. Take a moment to assess your level of exhaustion and stress. If you think this is the reason you're putting off the habit, then there are ways to deal with it.

2. IF YOU'RE TIRED, CAN YOU GET MORE REST? This is the best way to deal with exhaustion. Many people simply don't get enough sleep. They're running on high octane all day, then stay up late and don't have enough rest before starting another day full of motion. You can do this for a little while, but eventually the lack of rest will affect you—you'll start dragging, feeling lazy and burnt out, wanting to procrastinate. You might even get sick. The best thing is to get more sleep at night, so start going to bed earlier. A good nap also helps a lot. Even just 30 minutes, though an hour is better, if possible.

3. TAKE BREAKS. Get away from the computer, and take a walk. This is the best way to deal with stress—find ways to de-stress during the day. Stretch. Move around. Massage your neck and shoulders. Get some fresh air. Talk to someone in real life. Take a hot bath or shower if that's possible.

4. EXERCISE. I've found exercise to be one of the best ways to reduce stress. Ironically, it can be hard to start exercising if you're tired and stressed, but I've always felt a lot better after exercise, so it's worth putting some effort into starting. A fast walk, a good run, some strength exercises, a swim or bike, playing a sport. Not only does exercise reduce stress, but it helps you to sleep better at night. While it's good to exercise regularly, it's also best to have at least one to two rest days a week.

5. GET THE OVERWHELM UNDER CONTROL. Sometimes you're stressed or overwhelmed because there's too much going on in your life or too much information coming in. To make this more manageable, make a list of all you have going on right now. Now see if you can eliminate or put a hold on a few of them—simply send an email or make a call and tell people you can't work on this right now. Make a short list of three to five tasks you can actually work on today, and focus on the first item only. One thing at a time.

6. REDUCE THE INFLOW. If you have information overload, see if you can reduce or eliminate some of the information coming in. Unsubscribe from things in email, RSS, Twitter, Facebook. Limit your time in these communication mediums to certain periods a day, so you can disconnect and focus.

7. BREATHE. Focus on your breath as it comes into your

body and then goes out. Relax your jaw. Smile. Slow down for a minute. Return your mind to your breath. Let your tensions go out with your breath. Remind yourself that all that you have going on ... doesn't matter that much. At the end of the day, life will go on. This breathing exercise is available to you at any time of day.

8. MAKE YOUR TASK YOUR MEDITATION. Just as the breathing exercise can help calm you down and return you to the present moment, so can working on a task. Close all programs and devices and notifications not necessary for working on your task, and be mindful as you work on the task. Notice your thoughts, breath, fingers tapping away on the keyboard, body as it becomes stressed or relaxed. This is a form of meditation, and you can do it for each task.

Take an assessment of your levels of stress, tiredness, and energy for doing the habit. Assess your commitment to the habit and see if anything needs to be adjusted. If you're tired or stressed or other things are taking priority, take a small step toward one of these solutions.

Making mistakes, guilt from failing

It's impossible to overstate how common this downward spiral of guilt is when people try to form habits, mess up, and then feel guilty or undisciplined because of messing up. You can get stuck in a quagmire of guilt, not wanting to admit it to anyone, not starting again because you feel so bad about it all.

The guilt can be more harmful than the failure, and stops you from doing the habit. Guilt is tough—it's an insidious feeling that we barely notice but that has such a strong effect on us. You have to learn to be aware of it, then let it go and counter it with something more positive. Tell yourself that when you slip and fall, it's just another lesson that will teach you to be better at change.

Take a longer view of things: a failure is just for a day or two, or perhaps a week... but that doesn't matter in the long term. Missing a few days makes almost no difference in the course of a year. Over a lifetime, one day means nothing, but what you do on the vast majority of days is what counts.

Guilt is short-term thinking. Brush yourself off after falling down, learn from the mistake, and get going again as soon as you're able. Get back on track, and you'll feel great.

Positive feedback of mistakes

Another idea is to see mistakes not as negative feedback that you're bad at the habit, but as positive feedback for learning. Mistakes means you're pushing into new ground and exploring something interesting—if you weren't, you wouldn't make mistakes.

See every mistake as an opportunity to learn, a thing that you can get better at, the feedback that's so crucial for improvement. And smile as you open yourself up to this improvement.

❀ PART III ❀
Quitting a Bad Habit

This section of the book is a short guide to how to quit a habit that isn't helpful, as opposed to forming a new habit, as we did in Part I. The two main differences are that when you quit a habit, you must 1) face additional struggle against the urges to do the old habit, and 2) create new, positive habits for each of the triggers of the old habit.

When to attempt to quit

Most people make the mistake of trying to tackle a quit too early, when they still haven't gotten good at forming habits. This is a good way to set yourself up for failure, and then to feel bad about it. It's like attempting to build a house before you've learned to hammer and saw.

I recommend forming new, positive habits that we talked about in the "How to choose a first habit" chapter at least three times before taking on a quit. Even better would be to have five successful new habits under your belt before trying to quit a habit, if you have the patience. This would give you the skills and confidence you need, and quitting a habit would be much easier because of it.

The biggest recommendation is not to take on a quit if you're still struggling with forming habits. Creating a new habit should seem fairly easy, like something you know how to do. If it does, you're ready to quit something.

Track your habit & triggers

When we formed a new habit, we found an existing trigger in our lives, and tried to bond the new habit to it with repetition. After a bunch of repetitions, the trigger-habit combo becomes more and more automatic. With old habits that you want to break, you already have triggers for your old habit. They're already automatic from years of repetition.

So the first thing you need to do, before you attempt to quit a habit, is track it for three days and try to write down every trigger for the habit. Carry around a small piece of paper and pencil, and make a tally mark each time you do the habit. For example, if you'd like to quit smoking, make a tally mark on the paper each time you smoke. This creates increased awareness of the habit.

Each time you write down a tally mark, think about what you did right before you did the habit (for example, right before you smoked, you ate dinner) or what the circumstances were (other people were smoking around you, so you smoked). These are your triggers. Make a list of your triggers below your tally marks.

Finally, write out a short text document that lists all your triggers. Next to each trigger, write down what need you think the habit is meeting for each of these triggers—see the chapter "Common needs & replacement habits" for more on this.

Come up with
replacement habits

Each bad habit meets some kind of need, or you wouldn't be doing the habit. The problem is that while the need is very human, the way you're attempting to meet that need is not as helpful as it could be. So you can come up with replacement habits to meet the need in a better way.

For each trigger and need, write down a positive replacement habit that will meet the same need. For example, for the trigger of stress and need of coping with stress, you might exercise, walk, or meditate. For the trigger of meetings (and the need of dealing with the stress of the meeting), you might write down all your notes from the meeting, including action steps.

You'll want to find new ways of coping with common difficulties. For loneliness, you might try to exercise, write, teach yourself a new skill, or meet new people. If you're bored, you might cope by learning something new, or tackling a new challenge. These are just a few examples, but you can see that these are much healthier ways of coping.

Make a list of the new habits you'll form for each trigger. You don't need to form them all at once, if there are too many ... we'll talk about that in the "Gradual change vs. cold turkey" chapter.

Common needs & replacement habits

As a quick reference for the habits and triggers you might work on in the future, here are some very common needs that bad habits might fulfill, and some replacement habits to consider to meet those needs. You'll note that some replacement habits are repeated often, because they might help cope with multiple needs. And of course, there are many other possible needs and replacement habits—this is just to get you started.

Common needs are coping with the following:

1. Stress or anxiety
2. Exhaustion or tiredness
3. Boredom
4. Loneliness
5. Feeling bad about yourself or your life
6. Social anxiety
7. Feeling incompetent
8. Feeling out of control
9. A need for love or affection
10. A need for comfort
11. Needing a break

Ideas for replacement habits that might help with coping with many of these things include:

- Exercise
- Taking a walk
- Meditation
- Naming and staying with the feeling (a form of meditation)
- Talking with someone
- Taking a shower or bath
- Yoga
- Drinking tea mindfully
- Taking a break
- Massaging your own shoulders
- Taking a nap
- Getting some sunlight
- Drinking some water
- Journaling/writing
- Listening to music
- Reading a book
- Sketching practice
- Practicing a new skill
- Taking up a new hobby

Again, these lists aren't exhaustive, but they should get you started.

Recommended coping method

If you're willing to take on a challenge, an expansion of the meditation method mentioned in the list above is my recommended method for coping. Here's what you do: when you're feeling stress, anxiety, boredom, loneliness, etc. . . . just pause and turn your attention to this feeling. Be curious and really see how it feels, where it is in your body, what the quality of the feeling is. Become intimate with it, without trying to avoid it. It's a staying of the groundlessness we talked about in Part I. Watch it gently, without judgment or wishing the feeling weren't there. Treat it like a friend, kindly. And see that this feeling is impermanent, just arises but will pass, like a cloud. This is the whole meditation: just watch with curiosity and kindness, not attaching to the feeling or needing to act on it. I can't guarantee what results you'll get, but I urge you to explore this method. We'll talk more about it in Part IV of this book, on life struggles.

Use techniques you've learned

The good news is that if you've worked through several habits using the techniques from Part I of this book, you already have most of the skills you need to form your replacement habits from the last chapter. The techniques are mostly the same: repeat the new habit after the trigger a bunch of times, and after awhile, the new habit becomes automatic.

Some of the things you should do to form replacement habits that you've already learned:

1. Make a vow.
2. Put up visual reminders to do your new habit—written notes around where the trigger happens.
3. Do the new habit mindfully, and enjoy it.
4. Find gratitude as you do the new habit.
5. Notice your resistance, stay with the groundlessness.
6. Flow around disruptions and missed days.
7. Reflect on your learning and obstacles, and make adjustments.

These should be done for each new replacement habit, and you should review the chapters in Part I as you form each new habit, to ensure that you remember the instructions for each technique above. Forming these new habits is doable, if as with your previous habits, you take it slowly, take it seriously, and give it your full focus.

Gradual change vs. cold turkey

There are a couple very different ways to tackle a quit—with gradual change, or quitting all at once (the "cold turkey" method). I went cold turkey when I quit smoking, but I've used the gradual method to change my diet (quit eating junk food and other foods that weren't helping me, one at a time) and other behaviors. Let's briefly look at each, and then see when you might want to do each method.

GRADUAL METHOD: One version of this method is to gradually cut back on how much you do your old habit—smoke fewer and fewer cigarettes each day, have fewer drinks of alcohol, go on social media fewer times each day. This is now recommended by psychologists I know who specialize in addictions. But the method I would recommend is changing one trigger at a time—if you want to stop smoking after meetings, for example, form a new replacement habit for that trigger for a couple weeks before moving to the next trigger. This method takes patience, obviously, but in my experience (with food habits), it yields good results.

COLD TURKEY: This is just stopping completely with the bad habit, with all triggers at once. The benefit is that this can yield faster results, if you are able to fully focus on this and overcoming cravings and urges. It requires you to completely change your environment for awhile (get rid of all junk food, avoid trigger fast food places and social occasions, have support for your new healthy diet, etc.), and it isn't easy. Lots of people fail at this method and feel undisciplined as a result.

So which method should you choose? I highly recommend the gradual approach for most people, as I think it's much more likely to be effective. The cold turkey approach can work, if you're able to fully change your environment and give this change your full focus for at least a month, and if you don't have the patience to do the gradual method. I recommend patience.

Struggling with urges

The biggest difficulty with changing long-held bad habits is struggling with the urges to do the old habit. Your mind will constantly try to get you to do the habit, will want to give in to strong urges, will rationalize and otherwise try to do everything it can to talk you into doing the old habit.

Usually we just give in to the urges without thinking. But you can learn to be vigilant. Learn to recognize the urges as they arise. Instead of acting on them immediately, delay. Just pause, and watch them rise and fall, without acting. Delay again. Breathe. Walk around. Drink some water. Call someone for help. Go for a long walk. Get out of the situation. The urge will go away, if you just delay.

The right mindset also helps. If you allow yourself to listen to the rationalizations ("I deserve a break, this one time") or negative self-talk ("I can't do this"), you'll fail. See the rationalizations and negative self-talk, but don't believe any of it. Have a positive answer for each rationalization. Tell yourself you can do this, you're strong, you got this. And be realistic in that things won't go as planned, but those are learning opportunities. In the long run, you're going to make it, because you're worth it.

What happens when you fail

Most quits are not clean, but messy. There are slipups, there are urges that we follow, there are rationalizations that we give in to. The real question isn't whether you'll mess up, but what you'll do if you do mess up.

The skill to practice is to get back on track if you mess up, and to not let it derail you. Take mistakes in stride, and take the long view that what really matters is not whether you mess up for a day or two, but what you do over weeks and months and years.

Learn from any mistakes you make. Forgive yourself for any transgressions. See what happened, figure out a better plan for next time. Journal about it so you solidify your learning. You will get better and better as you learn from mistakes. In this way, mistakes are helping you improve your habit skills.

Types of quits

I'm going to assume you'd like to do one of the versions of the gradual method, and I'd like to give some recommendations for how to do that for specific types of quits.

FOOD CHANGES: If you want to quit eating junk food or stop overeating (for example), these can be difficult changes, because we have lots of food triggers. Track your triggers over time, because some of them don't come up every day—being at a family gathering, going out for drinks with friends, feeling really lonely, being stressed out by a work project. Figure out what need food is meeting (a way to lessen social anxiety, a way to bond with others, giving you a feeling of love, relieving stress) and see if you can find replacement habits for each trigger that meets these needs. For example, for the trigger of family gatherings, you might come up with games you can all play that meets the need of bonding. Know that food changes can take awhile to enact, because we have been doing our old habits so many years, usually dating back to childhood or teen-age years.

SMOKING: This is another habit that is used to deal with a lot of different difficult situations (awkward social situations, stress, anger, loneliness, long meetings), and so we need to figure out what situations or triggers cause the urge to smoke, and what needs they're meeting, and find another habit to cope with these situations. When I quit smoking, I liked to cope with stress by doing physical things, like take a walk, go for a run, do pushups, massage my own shoulders (to relieve stress), and meditate. Cutting back on the number of cigarettes, and using nicotine replacement, are often recommended methods as well.

INTERNET DISTRACTIONS: We turn to online distractions, like reading online or social media, often to avoid something difficult or otherwise uncomfortable. It's a way of coping with the difficulty of hard work or focus. To start, as always, we need to track our triggers, figuring out what happens just before we go to online distractions. Then perhaps find replacement habits, like getting up and walking around, doing a few pushups, writing in a journal, etc. Another replacement habit: staying with the difficult task despite the desire to move away from it, at least for five minutes, before taking a quick walking break. It's a good idea to limit your Internet distractions to certain times of the day, and have other times of day be non-distraction time, for focus, reflection, being disconnected, or creating. There will be lots of times when you mess up and go to distractions despite your best intention—in that case, write down your trigger and see if there's a need that the distractions are fulfilling, and find a replacement habit. Learn from the mistakes and try some of the strategies in the Troubleshooting section. Another good strategy is to take a week-long sabbatical from your top Internet distractions (social networks, blogs, news sites, etc.) while you form a replacement habit. When the sabbatical is over, to find a good balance, you might set certain times when you allow yourself to go to these distractions, rather than allowing yourself to do them all day.

TV WATCHING: While there's nothing wrong with watching good television, we can often use TV or video watching as a form of distraction, as a coping mechanism for boredom, stress, loneliness, exhaustion, not wanting to do uncomfortable or difficult work, etc. If this is a habit you want to reduce or quit (I suggest reducing instead of cold turkey), then you'll want to track your triggers and needs, find replacement habits that meet the needs, and focus on one of those replacement habits at a time. Another useful strategy, as with Internet distractions, is taking a sabbatical. The long-term key is finding a good amount of TV watching that works for you—an hour or so at the end of the day fits in with many people's lives, for example.

IMPULSE SHOPPING: Lots of people relieve stress or get doses of pleasure from going shopping, either in stores or online. Buying something on impulse can become a habit, surrounding us with more things we don't necessarily need and putting us in debt. This can be a tough habit to change because it might not happen every day or at predictable times. The key is to develop an awareness of your urge to buy something by making a tally mark on a piece of paper every time you go to a shopping site or physical store. Write down what you were doing or how you were feeling just before that happened—that's probably your trigger. Often shopping fulfills a need for comfort, love, stress relief, a feeling of control, a wanting to be a better/cooler/more attractive person. Replacement habits that help with that include talking to other people, taking a bath or drinking tea, doing yoga, journaling. Also try meditating on whether the purchase will really make you a better person, and whether you can find joy in the present moment without the purchase. You might try a 30-day shopping moratorium, where you don't allow yourself to buy anything new (other than food, toiletries, other necessities), while tracking your triggers and trying to form replacement habits.

NEGATIVE THINKING: Thinking habits can be very hard to change, because we're usually not aware we're doing them, and they're harder to notice than physical habits. It's easier to see when you're smoking or eating junk food than when you're thinking negative things about yourself. So the key, as always, is forming an awareness of the habit and triggers. Keep a journal, write a brief entry in it when you notice these thoughts. You might spend a few minutes in the morning just watching your thoughts, noticing patterns. I don't recommend working on this habit until you've done one or two other quits, so that you'll be reasonably competent at the skills you need before tackling something this difficult. It's important to note that this habit won't change overnight, but is something that could take months or years, to slowly improve. A good replacement habit is to notice your negative thoughts (about yourself, others, life), and stay with that feeling for awhile, before trying to give yourself love. A recommended book on this topic is Radical Acceptance by Tara Brach.

ALCOHOL OR DRUGS: To be honest, I don't have enough experience with severe substance addiction to give advice, and I highly recommend seeking professional treatment or counseling if you have a serious addiction. That said, it's still a good idea to understand your triggers, the emotional needs you're meeting with the drugs or alcohol, and to try to begin to cope with those needs in healthier ways. Gradual reduction of the substance is often recommended, to help with withdrawal symptoms. Professional support would make your chances of success at changing these habits much more likely.

There are, of course, many more habits that people would like to quit. The purpose of this chapter was to give you some ideas, and to illustrate the ideas for a successful quit through these common examples.

❀ PART IV ❀
Life Struggles

This section aims to apply some of the ideas we learned in Part I to struggles we might have in life: frustrations, unhappiness with ourselves, dealing with major life changes, uncertainty. As with the rest of the book, I won't dive deeply into why we have these struggles, but instead will go straight to recommended actions.

The heart of our struggles

We all get frustrated with ourselves, our lives, other people. We become disappointed, anxious, full of uncertainty. But why? What's going on?

There are two helpful ways of looking at why we struggle:

1. WE STRUGGLE WITH OUR MIND MOVIES. We have an image, a story, about how other people should act, how our lives should be, how we should be ... and this image conflicts with how all of these things actually are. We might also resist changes in our lives, resist things not going our way, which are two other ways we don't want things as they are. Our Childish Mind wants its way and is attached to the Mind Movie, so we resist how things actually are. This attachment to what we want, and resistance to the way things actually are, causes the struggle.

2. WE STRUGGLE WITH OUR FEELINGS. We might feel frustration, anger, uncertainty, fear, confusion, guilt, tiredness ... and these are perfectly natural feelings. They are all forms of groundlessness we reflected on in Part I. But we don't want to feel this groundless-

ness, these difficult feelings, so we avoid them. We try to find solid ground, often through bad habits and distraction. This avoidance of groundlessness is what causes the struggle.

These are both ways of looking at the same thing: we don't like the actuality of what's going on, and so we struggle with it. We are causing our own struggle. The good news is that we can let go of the struggle, with practice, and relax into the nature of reality in front of us.

That might mean relaxing into the basic goodness of ourselves. It might mean relaxing into the basic goodness of every moment. It might mean relaxing into the basic goodness of others who aren't behaving the way we think they should. In the end, with practice, we might develop a trust in the goodness of each moment, which includes us and everyone else.

This is the beauty of working with our struggles, rather than avoiding them. We can see deeper into reality and uncover the love that's already there.

Relaxing our struggling

We don't like experiencing difficult feelings (anger, frustration, anxiety, fear, uncertainty) or groundlessness, so we try to avoid the feeling. We seek distractions, food, shopping, drugs, smoking, busy-ness. Anything to find more familiar solid ground, and avoid the groundlessness.

This avoidance often leads to more struggles. It makes things worse. What if instead, we face the feelings? Invite these feelings to tea. Welcome them, get to know them. This method will help us deal with everything in life, so it's worth working on.

Here's how it works:

1. DEVELOP AWARENESS. We often don't even notice our difficult feelings, our groundlessness, because we're caught up in them. The first skill to develop is to recognize that you're having feelings of uncertainty, self-doubt, frustration, etc. Just notice, and name it. That might be all you work on at first.

2. SET AN INTENTION. When you recognize a feeling, try pausing to set an intention for working with this feeling. For example: "I will stay with my groundlessness to

be compassionate with myself." Or the intention might be compassion for another person.

3. INVITE IT TO TEA. See the feeling, then welcome it. Despite your wanting to avoid it, stay with the feeling. Be gentle and compassionate with it, as you would with a friend. Continue to stay with it for awhile.

4. USE GENTLE CURIOSITY. As you're staying with the feeling, observe it gently, without attaching to it. Give it respectful attention, noticing where the physical sensation is in your body. Explore it with gentleness. Observe how it feels, what the quality of the feeling is. Is it tightness in your chest, hollowness in your stomach, a shooting pain in your heart, a pulsing in your neck? Be curious, be gentle, explore.

5. RELAX YOUR STRUGGLES. Notice that there's a tightness around the feeling in your body and in your mind, because you don't want the feeling. Try to relax the part of your body where the feeling is—just loosen up, open up, create a little space around it, like a wide open expanse of field. Now relax the tension in your mind, as it resists this feeling. Loosen your struggle, relax into what is. Stop struggling, and open up some space.

6. LOOK WITHOUT IDEALS. Look honestly at yourself and this feeling, at everything around you, without ideals, without the Mind Movie of how you'd like things to be. Look at the reality, not who you want to be or ought to be, but with compassion at who you actually are, how things actually are. Loosen any attachment to your story, to the Mind Movie, and just see what's there.

7. MERGE INTO THE FEELING. As you loosen up your resistance to the feeling, relax into it, and bring your

awareness fully into it as it is ... you can begin to merge into it. You become the sensation. Only the sensation remains, no resistance to it or separation from it. The "me" who doesn't want the difficult feeling, the ground-lessness, is gone. And so you're free from pain and struggle. You might not experience this right away. We'll talk about it more in the next chapter.

This is an important method, but we don't learn it over-night. We might succeed with small difficulties, and not so much with bigger ones. We can grow this skill with repeated practice, so commit to practicing with whatever you face in your life, starting by just developing awareness of ground-lessness and difficult feelings.

Seeing and working
with true nature

Buddhists say that all of our struggles stem from being confused about the nature of reality. When we struggle with loss, it's because we want reality to be different than it is, more permanent, more like our Mind Movie. When we procrastinate, it's because we are avoiding the discomfort of groundlessness and want to find comfort, putting our comfort before all else. When we're frustrated with others, it's because we see things as a story with ourselves at the center. All of these are misguided notions of what reality is like, but if we stop to see what's really in front of us, these struggles can go away.

Some things to reflect on about reality:

1. IT'S IMPERMANENT. The true nature of life is change, impermanence. We struggle with that when someone dies, when we get sick, when we lose a job or a relationship changes ... but if we can accept this impermanence and embrace it, life becomes less of a struggle. Impermanence can be beautiful, like the gorgeousness of a plum blossom as it falls to its death. Each moment is fleeting, dewlike and beautiful, to be cherished. And then a new

beautiful moment arrives to be appreciated after that, a neverending everchanging stream.

2. WE'RE NOT SEPARATE. As we saw in the last chapter, with practice, we can merge our consciousness into our experience, so that difficult feelings (for example) aren't something to avoid ... because we become a part of them. We become our entire experience. Separation vanishes, and there isn't a "me" to be afraid for, a "me" to defend from others, a "me" to put above all else, because we're a part of the flow of life. This takes awhile to see, as you practice meditation, so don't expect this to click right away.

3. WE'RE NOT AT THE CENTER. We tend to see our Mind Movies with ourselves at the center of the story—I know I do, all the time. When I'm frustrated with someone, it's because they're not doing what I want, not treating me the way I want to be treated. But this frustration can be dropped if we learn to remove ourselves from the center of the story, learn to detach from the story itself. What is the alternative? To turn to the moment in front of us and see it as it is, without the story, without the ideals of the Mind Movie. To see that we're just a part of everything, not at the center. To see that other people are caught up in their stories, and don't have us at the center of their stories. To learn to love them for that, and love serving others instead of only ourselves. This love and being a part of something is much less of a struggle, and we find ourselves more at peace.

4. IT HAS A BASIC GOODNESS. Not everyone will agree, but I'll just share what I've seen in my investigations: there's a basic goodness in each moment,

underneath all of our struggles with groundlessness. We obscure this goodness with our stories, but if we can just open up to it, we can see it. As Pema Chodron says, "Through meditation practice, we realize that we don't have to obscure the joy and openness that is present in every moment of our existence. We can awaken to basic goodness, our birthright."

5. IT'S BEAUTIFUL, TO BE APPRECIATED. If there's beauty in the impermanence and basic goodness of life, it's also fleeting. At the end of my life, I'd like to say that I paid attention and appreciated the life that I was given. That I noticed its beauty, that I wasn't asleep the whole time.

6. WE CAN ASPIRE TO LOVE. When we take all of this in, the question becomes "how should I act?" And for me, the answer has been "love." If I aspire to love, if I put this at the forefront of my intentions and actions, I am happier. I act in a way that is whole-hearted, authentic, passionate and compassionate. I don't always succeed, but it's what I aspire to.

None of these facets of the true nature of life are easily seen, and it can take a lot of practice to see them and to remember them in daily life. Like anything, we get better with repeated practice.

Coping with loss

As I was publishing the first edition of this book, my dad died while visiting me for the holidays. It was the most painful loss I'd ever experienced. Then as I started writing this edition of the book, one of my best friends, Scott Dinsmore, died in a freak accident while climbing Mt. Kilimanjaro. It came as such a shock, and was another devastating loss for me.

I'm not going to pretend that the loss of loved ones is easy, because it never is. It's one of the most difficult things we have to deal with in our lives, and no method will stop the grief. Grief is natural and unavoidable when we face such difficult losses. The question isn't how to get rid of grief, but how to cope when we do have grief.

How to cope with loss

First, let yourself grieve. Don't block it out, don't think that you shouldn't. Just accept your grief as a part of your experience. This grief, too, is impermanent, and will pass like everything else, but it's here for now. See it as a stormy cloud over you, but accept the showers of pain that wash over your upturned face.

Next, turn mindfully toward your grief. With an intention of being compassionate with yourself, invite the grief to tea—welcome it instead of avoiding it, be gentle and compassionate with it. Stay with it, continue to stay, notice how it's a form of groundlessness that you've been practicing with. With a gentle curiosity, explore the feeling in your body, notice the sensation of it, become intimate with it.

As you're staying with your grief, notice the tightness in your mind and body around it, and see if you can relax your body and then your mind around this tightness. Give it some space, loosen the struggle. If you're inclined, see too if you can just merge into this feeling of grief, and become a part of it, so that there isn't a "me" who doesn't want to grieve, just the experience itself.

Then look below the groundlessness to the basic goodness of the current moment, with the love and grief that we're experiencing, this basic goodness in ourselves and everything around us that's there when we loosen our struggle and see what's in front of us.

Also reflect on the impermanence of life, and how we're struggling with accepting this basic fact of life, how we don't want the change that has come. Instead of resisting the impermanence, if we can accept and embrace it, let go of our ideal of what we want life to be, perhaps we'll struggle less.

Coping with life changes

Death of someone you love is just one kind of loss, though it is often the most severe. There are many other kinds of losses, both small and great:

- Loss of a job
- Loss of a home or car
- Loss from disaster
- Loss of a limb
- Loss of your youth
- Loss of a romantic relationship (breakup or divorce)
- Loss of a family (if your parents get divorced)
- Loss of your health.

Other life changes are also losses ... such as the loss of what we were used to, what we were comfortable with, how we saw ourselves. For example, if I quit my job to start a business, instead of being "Leo who had job security," I might become "Leo who doesn't know his financial future." Losses of identity like this can be very difficult to deal with.

Some other life changes you might be facing:

- Starting a new job or career
- Starting a new business or venture
- Starting a project that scares the crap out of you
- Being diagnosed with a major illness
- Suffering a major injury
- A loved one getting a major illness
- Moving to a new home
- Losing everything in a natural disaster
- Going to a new school
- Transitioning to a new role in your job
- Transitioning to a new phase in life
- Becoming a parent
- And so on

Major life changes include anything that takes a major shift in mindset, that gets you out of your comfort zone in a drastic way, that forces you to change how you see yourself, that scares and confuses you and fills you with uncertainty.

What we need to recognize is that these all come with the feeling of groundlessness that we've discussed and worked with. And so the method for coping with these various forms of groundlessness is the same:

1. SEE THE GROUNDLESSNESS, INVITE IT TO TEA. Recognize that the difficulties you're having with this change in your life is groundlessness, and that you're struggling with it, not wanting to feel it. Instead of avoiding, welcome it, stay with it with a compassionate attitude.

2. EXPLORE WITH CURIOSITY. Stay with the feeling, and explore it, get to know it, feel where it is in your body.

3. RELAX YOUR STRUGGLES. Notice the tightness in your body and mind around the feeling, and start to relax both, one at a time. Relax your struggles, and just be with the feeling. Hold less tightly to the ideal that you shouldn't have this feeling.

4. MERGE INTO THE FEELING. See if you can remove the separation you have with the feeling, and just become it. In this step, the "me" that doesn't want the feeling disappears.

5. EMBRACE THE IMPERMANENCE. As much as we'd like to have things stay the same, have control over things, it's not the way of the world. We can embrace the impermanence, accept the change, relax into it.

6. SEE THE BASIC GOODNESS. We can see that once we relax our struggle, we uncover the basic goodness in ourselves, the basic goodness available in every moment if we just allow ourselves to appreciate it.

I'm not saying that this method will end all struggles, and make everything bright and cheerful. But we can struggle less, with practice, when we face these struggles instead of avoiding them or wishing they weren't there.

Dealing with frustrations
with others

We all get frustrated with other people, often multiple times. We think, "If only they could see things my way, if only they could behave in the right way, if only they could do things my way ..." But they don't want to do things our way.

I've learned to respond with a little bit less frustration after reading something from Charlotte Joko Beck, author of *Everyday Zen*. Beck wrote: "The other person is never the problem."

The kids I'm frustrated with aren't the problem. They're going to behave imperfectly. The problem is my Mind Movie, my ideal, that they should behave considerately and quietly, not make mistakes, never make messes. In other words, I somehow have an ideal that they won't behave like human beings, and I am tightly attached to that deal. This attachment causes me to struggle with how things are, with how they're behaving, instead of accepting that people will behave imperfectly.

It's difficult to accept that the other person isn't the problem, because it really does seem like the other person is wrong. But consider this: other people will act in less-than-ideal ways every day, often multiple times a day. This is the reality. If we get angry every time someone else behaves imperfectly, we will constantly be angry. That's not a prescription for happiness.

However, while we can't control the other person's actions . . . we can change our own reaction. We can cope with our feelings with frustration and relax the struggle, as we have worked on in previous chapters. I won't go into detail about the method again—just refer to previous chapters for how to invite your groundlessness to tea, to become curious about it and intimate with it, to relax the struggle.

If we can react in a calmer, more peaceful manner, we will be happier. We will then act in a more compassionate way, smile, and perhaps the other person will be transformed just a little bit by this act of compassion.

This doesn't mean we ignore the other person's behavior or don't address the situation in front of us. It just means that we respond appropriately, out of a desire to make things better rather than out of anger or frustration, or from a desire to teach the other person a lesson or show that we're right. There will always be problems with other people, but we can get angry and act out of anger, or we can cope with our anger and groundlessness, relax our struggles and act out of compassion. Once we're a bit calmer, we can respond appropriately: talk to them calmly about the situation, take the opportunity to help them try a better method, act with compassion, let go of trying to control the person and focus on your own business, set up a system that works even if people are careless, and so on.

What's missing from all of the appropriate responses is anger and frustration, which only make the situation worse. Inappropriate responses are caused by anger. We always respond better when we remove the anger, and respond calmly. Don't assume bad intentions. Just respond appropriately.

Coping with relationship problems

How do you cope with inevitable relationship problems?

First, you use our method for groundlessness when you feel the groundlessness of relationship problems—whether the relationship problem is with a significant other, your kids, friends, other family, co-workers. You invite the frustration/groundlessness to tea, be curious with it, get intimate with it, relax your struggle.

Next, you can take a look at the struggles of the other person, seeing them as they are without your ideals, finding gratitude for them, seeing their suffering and wishing them happiness.

Once you come to a place of peace about your relationship and the other person, you can now respond appropriately. How? There are many ways, including trying to:

· Be compassionate with them.
· Talk to them (without blame) about what you're going through.
· Understand what they're going through.
· Understand what needs they're trying to fulfill in this situation.

- Talk openly but without blame about the problem in communication and resolve it so that you're both happy.
- Admit your contribution to the problem.
- Help them feel accepted and not attacked.
- Swallow your pride and admit you're wrong.
- Give them a hug.
- Write them a letter, if talking becomes too hard.
- Fix the mistake, apologize, mend the relationship, figure out what went wrong and how we can prevent the mistake in the future.
- Do our best to help.

Those are just some ideas, of course. There are endless possibilities, but you can see that these are all reasonable, calm, peaceful actions that are appropriate to the situation.

Once you find a place of peace, the appropriate response becomes much easier to find. Dealing with relationship problems and frustrations with others can be a struggle, because we can't control how the other person sees us, understands the situation, or behaves. When things aren't going well, it can drastically affect our happiness. But with practice, and not a small amount of breathing, you can get better at letting go of your story about the other person, relaxing your struggle, and responding to the situation with calmness and peace.

Dealing with unhappiness
with ourselves

Changing our lives is theoretically easy to do —just do a simple habit after a trigger once a day. But we sabotage ourselves for some reason, struggling with the change, giving up when things seem uncomfortable. It turns out that the reason we sabotage ourselves is often that we are unhappy or dissatisfied with ourselves. We tell ourselves a story that often sounds like this: "You're not good enough. You can't do this. You should just give up." Or maybe, "This is too hard. You shouldn't make yourself suffer. You deserve a treat."

Why are we unhappy with ourselves, at some level? Because we don't meet our own ideals for who we should be. The reality of who we are doesn't match up with our Mind Movie about who we should be.

Here's what one reader said about herself: "I was stuck in my emotions, always feeling bad for myself, always feeling wrong and unhappy. I was unable to realize all the things I have and be grateful for them. I only think about how I am a little overweight. I felt bad in my body, ugly and unloved."

We live in constant disappointment with ourselves. We have many ideals for ourselves, but inevitably, we fail to meet them, all the time. We constantly fail ourselves, constantly fall short of what we hope we'll be, what we think we should be.

So what can we do about this unhappiness with our-selves? In her book, *Radical Acceptance*, mindfulness teacher Tara Brach suggests that we get out of this Trance of Un-worthiness by fully accepting everything about ourselves. Brach says that radical acceptance is "... accepting our human existence and all of life as it is. Imperfection is not our personal problem—it is a natural part of existing."

That means we learn to accept not only our imperfec-tions, but the feelings we have about ourselves, along with the aversion we have to those feelings. It's all a part of who we are, and we can learn to accept all of that, with practice.

The practice of learning to accept ourselves is the same practice we've learned to deal with all of our groundlessness: to be aware of the feelings we're having about ourselves, to invite these feelings to tea, to become intimate with how they feel in our bodies, to relax our struggles with them, to merge into them and remove separation from the experi-ence. I won't go into the details of this practice—read the first few chapters of this part of the book for more infor-mation.

Once we've practiced with these feelings about ourselves for awhile, the next thing to notice is that underlying all of our feelings about ourselves is a basic goodness that we have, always present but often covered up by our struggles. By relaxing the struggles, we uncover this goodness. It's our loving and compassionate selves that are causing the diffi-culties, actually: because we want to be loved and accepted and good people, we have ideals for ourselves (that we're not meeting). We must see all of our "faults" as an expression of our underlying love.

With time, we can learn to recognize this feeling of un-worthiness, and learn to work with it. We can begin to accept our feelings about ourselves, accept everything about our-selves, and love the compassionate goodness that is always there.

Uncertainty about life's path

Something we struggle with every single day is uncertainty about whether we're doing the right things, in the right way. We are on an uncertain path in life, always, and this causes us feelings of groundlessness. We seek to find more solid ground by looking for certainty about what we're doing—we want to find the perfect productivity system, the perfect morning routine, the perfect way to make coffee or tea, the perfect home, the perfect creativity habits, and more. Unfortunately, this certainty doesn't exist, so our constant seeking of certainty finds no answers.

What can we do about this constant uncertainty? We can continue our fruitless search for certainty, or we can learn to work with the uncertainty. This helps us deal with the feeling directly, rather than trying to alleviate it but never actually finding relief.

We work with uncertainty the same way we work with any kind of groundlessness: by noticing it and inviting it to tea, by staying with it and exploring the feeling in our body with curiosity, by relaxing around the feeling and merging into it.

Once we practice getting to know and relaxing around the feeling, we can look beneath the groundlessness to the goodness and love that's beneath: this person who wants some kind of certainty, optimization, perfection ... is just trying to find his or her way in a chaotic, groundless world. It's scary, and the search for certainty in any way is just a compassionate act of dealing with that fear. Beneath that fear is a person who has basic goodness, in every moment.

We can also learn to work with a world that is constantly shifting, that gives us no certain answers. We have to go through our day facing this uncertainty, and again, our first instinct is to look for ways to find certainty: to develop the perfect routine, the perfect computer setup, the best way to work, the best way to eat, and so on. We don't actually find the certainty, the perfect anything, but we can't seem to stop searching for it. Instead, we can learn to walk down an uncertain path.

Here are some steps you might try taking:

- RECOGNIZE THAT YOU'RE TRYING TO FIND CERTAINTY—good indicators include trying to avoid the activity (procrastination/distraction), doing an Internet search for how to do something, looking for a book on the topic, seeking assurances from others, making a list or system to control the uncertainty. Pause and notice the fear, anxiety, or tension you might have around this, and stay with it awhile, exploring it and then relaxing around it.
- SEE THE BASIC GOODNESS—not only in yourself, but in the moment, in the world around you, that's underneath your feelings of uncertainty and groundlessness. This goodness is always there, always available to us, if we relax our struggle.

- FIND YOUR BASIC INTENTION TO DO GOOD.
  Whatever activity you're uncertain about, find the
  deeper intention you have for this activity. It might be
  an intention to be compassionate with yourself, or to
  help others.

- TAKE A STEP TOWARD THAT INTENTION. This
  step will be uncertain, and that's OK. You will never
  find a certain path, so just move toward the intention
  uncertainly. This is scary. It's not easy. But you have it in
  you to be moved by your intention.

- BE CURIOUS. Explore this uncertain, groundless path
  with an open mind, a curiosity for how things actually
  are, rather than having to know the answers. Open your
  heart and mind, be inquisitive, question what you know,
  and see this as an opportunity to learn.

- EMBRACE THE CHANGE. A shifting ground can be
  seen as scary, uncertain, dangerous … or it can be seen
  as an opportunity for learning, growth, new knowledge.
  Think about what you're afraid might happen if you
  don't have certainty, and see the good that can happen
  as well. See that there's freedom in this uncertainty,
  because your path isn't determined, and you can explore
  all kinds of paths. Learn to embrace the shifting path,
  and become adaptive, flexible, responsive, fluid, open,
  with practice.

- PRACTICE IN SMALL DOSES. When you're just
  starting out with uncertainty, it can be scary stuff.
  Try working in small doses, just a few minutes at
  a time, and allow yourself to grasp for certainty in
  some ways—developing a sacred space for writing or
  meditating, for example, is a way to build seemingly
  firm ground around a place to practice working with

groundlessness. You don't need to work with uncertainty all day long—just a little each day, and you'll get better and more confident of being able to handle bigger doses later.

· REFLECT, AND DEVELOP TRUST. As you take a few steps on an uncertain path, reflect afterward to see how it went. Did things turn out disastrously, or did they turn out fine? Did you learn anything? Through this practice, you begin to develop trust that each moment will turn out OK. Not that things won't go wrong, or that you won't ever have failure, but that even when things go wrong or fail, things are still OK. This trust in the moment is a great thing to develop over time.

I don't claim that any of this is easy, but grasping for solid ground when that doesn't exist isn't easy, either. Avoiding the uncertainty with distraction and procrastination seems easier, but it's not a path to happiness or learning. Working with the uncertainty is a much richer ground for exploration.

PART V

Just Do This

This section was inspired by Derek Sivers, who wrote a great blog post about compressing wisdom into simple directives. His observation is that most people don't want to read long explanations—they just want you to give them the "do this" directives, telling them what to do in simple language. That's what this part of the book is about: it simplifies everything in this book into simple "just do this" statements.

Simple plan to create new habits

To create a new habit, follow these steps for about six weeks:

1. PICK ONE NEW, EASY HABIT THAT YOU CAN DO ONCE A DAY: walking, a few pushups, meditating for a few minutes, writing a couple paragraphs, journaling, eating one vegetable. Only do one new habit at a time. Don't pick a habit that is difficult, and don't try to quit an old habit until you're good at forming new ones.

2. DON'T START RIGHT AWAY: Wait until you get to Step 6 before actually doing the habit— the first five days should be spent thinking over the first step above, and the next few steps. Anticipation of starting the habit, without starting it, is a good idea.

3. CREATE A VOW: Take a day to consider your intention with this new habit. Why are you doing it? Does this reason feel important to you, connected to one of your deeper purposes? Is it a compassionate act for yourself or others? Understand your deeper intention. Now make a big commitment to yourself—be all in, and vow not to let yourself down. Write this vow down

somewhere you can see it each day, and honor yourself by sticking to this vow to your utmost ability.

4. CREATE A SPACE: Even though we're going to start small (see Minimum Viable Habit in Step 6), you should block off 10 minutes in your day to focus on your habit. Make it a priority, an unmissable appointment, so that you can stick to your vow.

5. SET A TRIGGER & REMINDER: Pick something to tie your habit to, something you already do every day—for example, morning coffee, opening your laptop, taking a shower, brushing your teeth, waking up, getting to work, getting home from work, eating breakfast or lunch or dinner, going to bed. This daily event will be your trigger, and you'll want to do your habit right after the trigger (with no delay) every day. Put up a note where your trigger happens (near the coffeemaker if the trigger is coffee) so you remember to do the habit.

6. START WITH A MINIMUM VIABLE HABIT: Today, start doing your habit with the smallest version of your habit—just one minute or so, right after your trigger. It's important in the first week to start small, to overcome resistance and busy-ness that arise in the first few weeks. Try to mindfully enjoy the habit. You can go a bit longer after the minute is up, if you're still enjoying it and want to do a little more.

7. FOCUS ON ENJOYING THE HABIT: Notice the tendency to want to rush through your habit, and instead, try to slow down and enjoy the habit every day. Enjoy the learning process, and reflect on the sense of accomplishment when you're done doing the habit. Be grateful for doing the habit each day. The more you can give

yourself this positive feedback during the habit change process, the better.

8. PRACTICE MINDFULNESS: As you do your habit, try shining a spotlight of mindfulness onto the habit. Turn your mindfulness onto your breath, then your body, then your surroundings, then all the other sensations associated with the movements of doing the activity. Try to appreciate everything about doing the habit that you can. Enjoy those wonderful things about the habit so that the habit itself becomes your reward.

9. WATCH YOUR MIND MOVIE: Reflect on what story you're telling yourself about the habit—the ideal you have in your mind. What ideal or fantasy do you have about this habit? Now turn your attention to the reality of doing the habit, and be curious about what the habit is actually like.

10. REFLECT AND JOURNAL: Once a week, take a minute after you're done with the habit to reflect on how the habit has gone for you. What has it been like in reality, as opposed to the fantasy you had about it before you started? What have you learned? What do you appreciate? What obstacles have come up, and are there ways to overcome them as you continue? Consider writing a short journal entry about these reflections, to solidify the learning.

11. A DAILY PRACTICE: A process to practice each day you do the habit: set your intention, sense the energy of the moment as you do the habit, feel gratitude, and only quit on the third urge.

12. INCREASE GRADUALLY: Over the course of about six weeks, try to increase the length of the habit you do very slowly, just a little bit more each week. So if you

start with a minimum of one minute the first week, increase to two minutes the second week, then three the next, and so on. However, only increase if you didn't miss more than two days in a week.

This is the basic process of forming a habit. As you practice the mindfulness in Step 8 and watch your Mind Movie mentioned in Step 9, you might notice some resistance to doing the habit. See the next section for more on practicing with resistance.

If you have any difficulties, refer to Part II of this book on Habit Troubleshooting.

Finally, see the section after that on creating gradual life change, for more on where to go after your six weeks of doing this habit is over.

Practice with resistance & groundlessness

As you go through the first six weeks of doing a new habit, or you try to quit a bad habit, you are likely to find your mind resisting the change. This is normal—our minds resist a lot of things that we don't want or are not used to. With your habit change, or with anything in life, practicing mindfulness with your resistance is a good thing.

Here are some things I recommend:

1. NOTICE YOUR RESISTANCE: Watch for any resistance you have doing the habit, or reflect on recent resistance you've seen. If you see the urge to do something else, this is the Childish Mind putting up resistance to discomfort. If you've been struggling, resisting, uncomfortable, feeling disappointed, feeling uncertainty, feeling like quitting … these are some forms of dissatisfaction (or "groundlessness").

2. QUIT THE THIRD TIME: Try staying with your feelings of resistance or dissatisfaction for awhile, instead of avoiding them. Notice how you'll want to switch your attention to something else instead of staying with the feeling. But instead of switching, stay a little longer.

The next time you feel like switching, stay a little longer. Then on the third urge to quit, go ahead and quit. Try doing this "quit on the third time" practice all week if you can.

3. BE CURIOUS: What does the resistance or dissatisfaction feel like, as a physical sensation in your body? Where is it located, what is the quality of the sensation? Explore it with curiosity. Get to know this feeling, become intimate with it.

4. RELAX THE STRUGGLE: As you explore this feeling in your body, notice the tension you have in your body and mind around having this feeling in you. Relax your body around the feeling, just loosen up a bit, open up some space in you. Now relax your mind around this feeling. Allow yourself to struggle less.

5. RECONNECT WITH YOUR WHY: Pause for a moment to remember your intention for this habit, your deeper reason for doing it. The more often you can set your intention before doing the habit, the better. Reconnect with your gratitude for being able to do this habit, with the simple enjoyment of the action.

6. PRACTICE BEING OK IN GROUNDLESSNESS: Do you have uncertainty, dissatisfaction, frustration, fear? Again, these are forms of groundlessness (the ground being pulled from under you), and our first reaction is to run from this feeling. Practice being OK with this uncertainty, being OK with the discomfort, and just seeing what that's like. Find ways to be grateful for being in this state. See that you're OK even with this feeling inside you. See that this moment, even with groundlessness, is enough. See the basic goodness inside yourself,

and in this moment, that's there underneath all the groundlessness.

It is useful to practice with groundlessness not just for habits, but for all kinds of difficulties in life. It describes any feeling of not having solid ground under your feet, for example when you lose your job or a loved one dies, and you feel like the rug has been pulled out from under you. And in fact, this happens to us all the time, in big and small ways. It's a feeling we all have, and try to avoid. I recommend practicing with the feeling often, using these steps.

Create gradual life change

If you've started to solidify a habit, you might consider creating other new habits. You might also wonder about how to change many things in your life—more than just one small change. Here are some recommendations:

1. CONSIDER A SECOND HABIT: If your first new habit is starting to become ingrained, you might be eager to start a second habit. It's usually a mistake to try to do two habits at once, but once one habit has become fairly automatic and part of your new "normal," you can think about a second habit. For your second habit, I recommend another daily, positive habit that is very meaningful to your deeper purposes. Don't quit a bad habit yet, until you've successfully formed several good habits.

2. THE SLOW CHANGE METHOD: If you did your first habit in a very easy, tiny way ... you'll know what it's like to start out easy and only progress gradually. This is the Slow Change method—instead of revamping your entire diet all at once, imagine adding one vegetable to it for a few weeks, then another vegetable, then a fruit, then some nuts, and slowly, gradually, over time ... your

entire diet is different. It's gradual, so you barely notice the difference, and your mind hardly objects. You
can change your entire life using this Slow Change
method—consider what tiny changes you can make
over the next few months that will be easy to make but
meaningful in the long term.

3. LET GO OF UNHELPFUL CHANGES: This method
sometimes means letting go of habit changes that
haven't worked out well. It can be disappointing to let
go of a habit you had such high hopes for, that you've
worked so long for, but we have to remember that we do
these habit changes to learn about ourselves. Consider
whether your new habit has been as helpful as you'd pictured, and whether it's worth carrying it forward. If not,
give yourself permission to drop it, and perhaps revisit
the habit later.

4. REFLECT & ADJUST: If you decided to keep your
habit going, take a few minutes to consider how it's
gone so far, what you've learned, and what obstacles
you've encountered. What adjustments do you need
to make? What have you learned that can be applied
to future habits? Write a short journal entry to solidify
these learnings.

5. GO INTO HABIT MAINTENANCE MODE: As you
prepare to take on a second habit, your first habit should
be getting more automatic, not needing reminders,
more a part of your "normal." Put your first habit into
"habit maintenance mode," continuing to do the habit
but with less focus. You don't need to keep track of it
every day. Every few days, pause and reflect on your first
habit and check in to see that everything is still going
well. Maybe once a week, use one of these reflections

to assess whether you have any obstacles around the first habit, whether you need to make adjustments, whether there's anything new you've learned. After awhile, you'll need to reflect on the habit less often.

6. START YOUR SECOND HABIT WITH AN ADJUSTED METHOD: For your second habit, you'll want to follow the steps outlined in the "Simple plan to create new habits" chapter ... but you can adjust the method based on the obstacles you faced in the first habit. If you had a hard time with something and found a good solution (say, public accountability), you'll want to try that solution with your second habit. Learn from the first attempt, and make your method better with each attempt.

7. EMBRACE THE UNCERTAIN PATH OF CHANGE: The gradual changing of your life won't be a straight path, ordered and neat. It will be messy, littered with failed habits, constant stops and restarts. There isn't an optimal path, no certainty that you're doing it right. So toss out the ideal of a plan that has certainty and precision, and instead embrace the uncertainty of not knowing what you're doing. See if you can stay in this place of uncertainty, continue to walk down the path of habit change without anyone telling you it's the right way, and be OK with it. Embrace the uncertain path with curiosity.

Quitting a bad habit

To quit a habit that isn't helpful, as opposed to forming a new habit, you'll need to face additional struggle against the urges to do the old habit, and create new, positive habits for the triggers of the old habit. Here are my recommended steps:

1. DON'T ATTEMPT A QUIT UNTIL SEVERAL SUCCESSFUL NEW HABIT CHANGES: Most people make the mistake of trying to tackle a quit too early, when they still haven't gotten good at forming habits. This is a good way to set yourself up for failure. Form new, positive habits at least three times before taking on a quit; five is even better. Most important: Don't take on a quit if you're still struggling with forming habits. Creating a new habit should seem fairly easy.

2. TRACK YOUR HABIT: Before you attempt to quit a habit, track your habit for three days and try to write down every trigger for the habit. Carry around a small piece of paper and pencil, and make a tally mark each time you do the habit. This creates increased awareness of the habit.

3. LIST YOUR TRIGGERS: Each time you write down a tally mark, think about what you did right before you did the habit or what the circumstances were. These are your triggers. Make a list of your triggers below your tally marks.

4. LIST YOUR NEEDS: Write out a short text document that lists all your triggers, and what need you think the habit is meeting for each of these triggers. Each bad habit meets some kind of need. See the chapter on "Common needs & replacement habits" in Part III for more. Write these needs down for each trigger.

5. COME UP WITH REPLACEMENT HABITS: For each trigger and need, write down a positive replacement habit that will meet the same need. You'll want to find new ways of coping. The chapter on "Common needs & replacement habits" also has more on this. Make a list of the new habits you'll form for each trigger. You don't need to form them all at once.

6. USE TECHNIQUES YOU'VE LEARNED: To form your new replacement habits, use the same techniques you used to form new habits. Make a vow; put up visual reminders where the trigger happens; do the new habit mindfully, focusing on enjoyment; find gratitude as you do the new habit; notice your resistance and stay with the groundlessness; reflect on your learning and obstacles, and make adjustments. Do this for each new replacement habit, and review the chapters in Part I as you form each new habit.

7. GRADUAL CHANGE VS. COLD TURKEY: You can either quit a bad habit all at once ("cold turkey") or do it gradually. The gradual method is to either gradually cut back how much you do your old habit (smoke

or drink a little less each week) or create one new replacement habit for one trigger at a time. The gradual method takes more patience but yields good results, while the cold turkey method takes much more focus, energy, and determination. Lots of people fail at the cold turkey method, and unfortunately feel undisciplined as a result. I highly recommend the gradual methods for most people.

8. STRUGGLING WITH URGES: The biggest difficulty with changing long-held bad habits is struggling with the urges to do the old habit. Your mind will constantly try to get you to do the habit, will rationalize as much as it can. Usually we just give in to the urges, but you can learn to be vigilant. Learn to recognize the urges as they arise, and instead of acting immediately, delay. Just pause, and watch them rise and fall, without acting. Delay again. Breathe. Walk around. Drink some water. Call someone for help. Go for a long walk. Get out of the situation. The urge will go away, if you just delay.

9. FORM THE RIGHT MINDSET: If you allow yourself to listen to the rationalizations ("I deserve a break, this one time") or negative self-talk ("I can't do this"), you'll fail. See the rationalizations and negative self-talk, but don't believe any of it. Have a positive answer for it: tell yourself you can do this, you're strong, you got this.

10. WHEN YOU FAIL: Most quits are not clean, but messy. We give in to rationalizations. If you do mess up, the skill to practice is to get back on track and to not let it derail you. Take mistakes in stride, take the long view. Learn from any mistakes you make. Forgive yourself for any transgressions. See what happened, figure out a better plan for next time. Journal to solidify your learning.

Deal with life's difficulties

I recommend reading through the chapters in Part IV of this book, on life's difficulties, but basically we look at the reason we struggle in life, and talk about a method for dealing with that. The method draws from some of the things we learned in the sections on forming habits. Here it is in brief:

1. WE ALL STRUGGLE: Every one of us has to deal with frustrations, uncertainty, fears, unhappiness with ourselves, dealing with major life changes, frustrations with other people, disappointments, anxiety. These are all forms of groundlessness.

2. WE STRUGGLE WITH OUR MIND MOVIES. We have a story—about how other people should act, how our lives should be, how we should be ... and that conflicts with how these actually are. We often resist changes in our lives, resist things not going our way. Our mind wants its way, is attached to the ideal. This attachment to what we want, and resistance to what is, causes the struggle.

3. WE STRUGGLE WITH OUR FEELINGS. We don't want to feel this groundlessness, these difficult feel-

ings, so we avoid them, try to find solid ground, often
through bad habits and distraction. This avoidance of
groundlessness is what causes the struggle.

4. SEE THE GROUNDLESSNESS, INVITE IT TO TEA.
Recognize that the difficulties you're having with this
change in your life is groundlessness, and that you're
struggling with it, not wanting to feel it. Instead of
avoiding, welcome it, stay with it, using a compassionate approach.

5. USE GENTLE CURIOSITY. As you're staying with
the feeling, observe it gently, without attaching to it.
Give it respectful attention, noticing where the physical sensation is in your body. Explore it with gentleness, observing how it feels, what the quality of the
feeling is. Is it tightness in your chest, hollowness in
your stomach, a shooting pain in your heart, a pulsing
in your neck? Be curious, be gentle, explore.

6. RELAX YOUR STRUGGLES. Notice that there's a
tightness around the feeling in your body and in your
mind, because you don't want the feeling. Try to relax
the part of your body where the feeling is—just loosen
up, open up, create a little space around it. Now relax the tension in your mind, as it resists this feeling.
Loosen your struggle, relax into what is. Stop struggling, and open up some space.

7. LOOK WITHOUT IDEALS. Look honestly at yourself and this feeling, at everything around you, without ideals about how you'd like things to be. Look at
the reality, not who you want to be or ought to be, but
with compassion at who you actually are, how things
actually are. Loosen any attachment to your story, and
just see what's there.

8. MERGE INTO THE FEELING. As you loosen up your resistance to the feeling, relax into it, and bring your awareness fully into it as it is ... you can begin to merge into it. You become the sensation. Only the sensation remains, no resistance to it or separation from it. The "me" who doesn't want the difficult feeling, the groundlessness, is gone. And so you're free from pain and struggle. You might not experience this right away.

9. EMBRACE THE IMPERMANENCE. As much as we'd like to have things stay the same, have control over things, it's not the way of the world. We can embrace the impermanence, accept the change, relax into it.

10. SEE THE BASIC GOODNESS. We can see that once we relax our struggle, we uncover the basic goodness in ourselves, the basic goodness available in every moment if we just allow ourselves to appreciate it.

We can grow this skill with repeated practice, so commit to practicing with whatever you face in your life: the loss of a loved one, major changes in life, frustrations with others, uncertainty in your life path.

Finally: On love

We've gone through the learning path of creating new habits, struggling with them, being mindful of your ideals and frustrations. We've worked with the urges of bad habits, the resistance of our minds to change, the groundlessness that we try to avoid every day.

We've relaxed our struggles, and worked on letting go of our attachments to ideals. After letting go and relaxing, what are we left with?

We're left with love. There is an underlying boundless love in all of us, not for one specific person but for all living beings, for the world in general, that can motivate us to get up each day and do something good.

This love can motivate us to create great work, to be helpful to others, to be compassionate with ourselves by eating healthy food and being active, to work with our frustrations and groundlessness.

Love can move us to be mindful, to appreciate the reality of this current moment, to appreciate and embrace impermanence as something beautiful, to be grateful, to make the most of this dewlike life.

Love can move us to overcome struggles.

Love can transform bitterness into softness, anger into kindness, self-hatred into self-compassion.

Love is both the path, and the mover.

Love moved me to write this for you, and I hope that you will pass it on for me.

> *"We will develop love, we will practice it,*
> *we will make it both a way and a basis ..."*

BUDDHA

About the author

LEO BABAUTA writes about simplicity, habits, and mind-fulness on Zen Habits (zenhabits.net). He has changed many of his own habits and helped others change theirs.

He and his wife Eva, and their six kids, live a simple life in northern California. He prefers reading novels: Tolstoy, Joyce, Cervantes, Vonnegut, Fitzgerald, Lethem, Douglas Adams, Chandler, Ishiguro, Murakami, Rowling, Nabokov, William Gibson, Ann Patchett, Terry Pratchett.

Acknowledgements

It's impossible to thank everyone who supports you over the years. Just know that if I know and love you, and you're not listed here, you are deeply in my heart.

My lovely wife Eva has been my rock, and none of this would be possible without her. My mom's constant love and encouragement has always kept me going. My kids—Chloe, Justin, Rain, Maia, Seth, Noelle—are the reasons I do everything, and I love them more than I can say.

The deepest and weirdest part of my heart is eternally reserved for my brothers and sisters: Kat, Ana, Tiara, Joseph, Brandon, Austen.

I am blessed with incredible friends—Jesse, Tynan, Corbett, Susan, Dominic, Toku, among many others—who support me and inspire me and hold my feet to the fire.

My dad, Jose, died while I was publishing the first edition of this book, and I miss him every day. His creativity and humor were always sources of inspiration for me.

My grandfather, now deceased, was a hero to me, the reason I became a writer. My grandmother has been such a source of love and strength that a substantial portion of my heart is dedicated to her.

As I was writing the second edition of this book, my friend Scott Dinsmore died while climbing Mt. Kilimanjaro. It was an unbelievable tragedy, and I am deeply saddened by the loss of my wonderful friend. Scott, I miss you truly, love you, and am so grateful for your friendship.

And I can't express enough gratitude for you, my readers. You have changed my life profoundly.

Thank you, all of you.

This second edition was published in 2015 by Pipe Dreams
Publishing, written by Leo Babauta in Davis, California,
on airplanes to and from southeast Asia, in coffee shops in
Vietnam and Thailand; and improved with reader feedback.

Designed by Matt Avery (mattaverydesign.com);
cover painting by Lisa Class (lisaclass.co.uk);
author photo by Francisco Garcia Hrsitov (fghlux.com).

Book resources can be found at
http://zenhabitsbook.com/resources/

This book was set in Arno, a typeface designed by
Robert Slimbach in 2007, inspired by early humanist
typefaces from the 15th and 16th centuries.

Printed in Great Britain
by Amazon